after
THE BABY

Kathryn Voetberg

Copyright 2019 Kathryn Voetberg
All rights reserved.

"Lo, children are an heritage of the LORD: and the fruit of thewomb is his reward."
- *Psalm 127:3*

Dedication

To Leon and Lucy,
thank you for being my first
little boy and girl. It is an honor
to be your Mother.

Contents

Chapter 1: First Came Love — 1

Chapter 2: The Birth — 7

Chapter 3: Great Expectations — 11

Chapter 4: Communication — 31

Chapter 5: Rollercoaster: Emotions and Hormones — 41

Chapter 6: Sleep and Fatigue — 59

Chapter 7: Intimacy During Healing — 69

Chapter 8: We're Huge Fans of YOUR Family — 85

Chapter 1

First Came Love

I crouched underneath the trampoline with my 7-year-old sister, Kyla, and scrunched my freckled nose to see against the glaring summer sun.

"There he is. There's Elisha!" I whispered excitedly. All I could see were his tan legs sticking out of wide basketball shorts and disappearing into thick patriotic basketball shoes, but butterflies fluttered frantically in my stomach.

"His name isn't Elisha. It's "Pete." Kyla whispered back.

I never said one word to Elisha that weekend, but the moment I arrived home in Southern California from family camp in Oregon, I dug out my journal and scrawled as only an 8-year-old can, "I want to marry Elisha Peter Voetberg."

Seven years passed, and my stomach churned with anticipation each time we drove up to that annual family camp. Blood raced up and down my veins, as I peered through the car window and caught a glimpse of my suave, mysterious dream man. Each year he seemed a little tanner, a little more muscular, and a little more out of reach. I had a big fat crush on Elisha Voetberg . . . so did every other girl.

You see, Elisha was five years older. Every July my excitement would turn to nausea as I watched older girls with makeup, graceful curves, and actual phone numbers flocking to flirt with the broody musician and athlete. I stood to the side, hair stick straight, body stick straight, and a big gap between my front teeth. His friends could drive and mine still went to bed at eight o' clock. He would be snatched up long before I would be competition.

I've always liked to set myself up to win, and Elisha's heart seemed to be a losing battle, so around 15-years-old I gave up and moved on to other boys who loved my fiery spirit, quick wit, and gung-ho attitude. I wasn't just going to be "another girl" in the parade of ignored females trailing behind this distant charmer.

Enter my 18th birthday. I casually flipped open my computer to see an email from THE ELISHA PETER VOETBERG in my inbox.

"Ah!!!!!" I let out a small scream and then instantly stopped my welling excitement. Elisha barely knew my name. This was probably just my best friend (his kid sister) playing a trick on me.

Shakily, my hands found the mouse and clicked, "open." My heart beat so wildly I could hear it, and

I held my breath. This was real.

"AHHHHHHH!!! ELISHA WANTS TO GET TO KNOW ME!!!!" This time I screamed long and hard, running downstairs and bringing my ten siblings running with me to my parent's room. "Elisha Voetberg just emailed me! Tell me this isn't a joke!"

My father's startled eyes instantly told me he questioned this decision to let me start dating. If I had given him struggles with boys in the past, he was in for a whole new adventure when it came to Elisha. I was ready to march to the altar and say, "I do."

In the months that followed, our relationship was painfully long-distance and highly chaperoned due to my obsessive nature. Even though Elisha was 22, it was both of our first experience in a relationship. We were awkward, reserved, and constantly surrounded by our many siblings.

Because of my status as a "fan-girl" for so many years, I was uncharacteristically insecure around Elisha. I knew I was smart enough, pretty enough, and talented enough for many guys, but I felt so unsure around my idol.

It turns out, Elisha was unconfident too. Even though it appeared he had the world at his fingertips, Elisha questioned every move he made, and deep down, he was just as insecure. I waited for him to tell me he loved me. Apparently, he was waiting on me, and nine months later we ended our slow and torturous relationship of handwritten letters and rare group hang-outs.

A year and a half later, I was fresh off a breakup, road-tripping up to a wedding with two of my sisters and my best friend, Lilja Voetberg. Summer wind whipped through our hair and Taylor Swift blared through the speakers. As the hours flew by with singing and laughter, I nearly forgot that a month earlier, I honestly thought I was going to be engaged by now.

"Hey! I just got a text from Elisha."

I turned down the music and shot a glance at Lilja. "What's up?" Lilja's and my friendship had stayed intact, but we didn't really talk about her brother. Last I heard he was getting engaged.

"He's camping in Idaho and wants us to take him to the wedding. It's on our way," she shrugged.

Any old feelings I had for Elisha were faded memories, but for some reason, I jumped at the idea to road trip with him. I was curious about his life and interested in his rocky relationship. But when we pulled up at the coffee shop to pick him up, my stomach flip-flopped against my will. Elisha and I would never work out, but he was sure cute.

"So . . . tell us about your relationship," I laughed as I sat beside Elisha in the passenger seat. All my old insecurities around him were gone, and for the first time, I knew I was mature, seasoned, confident, and attractive. "We want to hear some drama."

"I broke up last night."

"What?! Again?" I teased.

"Seriously, it's for real this time," Elisha shrugged. "It just wasn't meant to be."

For the next several hours our three sisters chatted amongst themselves in the back seat, while Elisha and I had the first meaningful conversation of our lives—connecting over our recent pain. The trials of his last year and a half made him a man, and I didn't feel like a skinny kid anymore. He made me feel like a woman.

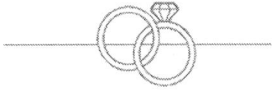

From there on out, our relationship was a hotbox of emotion, passion, arguments, and drama. With families to convince and my pedal to the metal personality, our tumultuous relationship seemed to be on the breaking point until the day I walked down the aisle. But that's a story for another time.

Let's suffice it to say that three weeks after we started dating, Elisha and I went ring shopping. Through it all, we knew we wanted each other. We knew we'd make a good team, and we were willing to work through anything to make that happen.

Best decision ever.

Three years and three babies later, we've worked through a lot of different challenges through changing seasons, and we continue to add more and more tools to our toolbox.

Working through challenges as a team is an incredible experience, and it builds so much unity in a relationship. I'm thankful for the rocky start that gave us the confidence to believe we can work through anything.

In this workbook, we are going to attack the five areas of postpartum that wreak the most havoc on our marriages after our precious children enter the world. However, this isn't just to tell you our story and share what worked and what DID NOT work for us. This is a workbook. A tool. It's only going to improve your marriage, if you take the time to do the exercises and talk through the hard stuff.

I have a feeling that's why you bought this. You WANT to experience greater intimacy with your spouse, and you want that postpartum season to be a challenge that draws you together, instead of tearing you apart.

Our goal is that this book will provide you with some tools to help you and your spouse work through the difficult hormones, miscommunication, pain, and fatigue surrounding postpartum.

You are a team. And embracing that truth is what's going to make "after the baby" a beautiful time.

Chapter 2
The Birth

Elisha:

Katie and I had just started with our practical preparation for the arrival of our first child.

We were less than three weeks away from our due date. Katie cleaned and organized our spare bedroom on Monday, cleaned the bathrooms on Tuesday, and organized the kitchen on Wednesday. We had plans to shop for supplies on Thursday and Friday. (We should have done the shopping on Wednesday.)

Our friends, Brook and Kent, were kind enough to bring us dinner on Wednesday night. We ate late, then stayed up even later having great conversation with them. Katie and I were both exhausted when we finally hit the pillows around 11:45 PM. I had been reading for about 15 minutes when Katie jumped out of bed and ran to the bathroom. She called me in to inform me that her water just broke. I wanted to believe her, but I thought for sure she was mistaken because we hadn't even done our supply shopping yet.

She wasn't mistaken. Her water had indeed broken. Game on.

Although I had never been present for any other birth in the history of my life, I responded like a seasoned veteran. Poised and confident. Naive and fearless. Unassuming and innocent....

Katie wasn't having any contractions so we decided to get some sleep. While I slept, Katie started to have contractions. According to Katie, the contractions were mild and manageable for the first four hours. That's what I would have said, too: mild and manageable.

At 5 AM, the contractions increased in intensity and frequency. I can attest to this. They were so dramatic they even woke me up. I quickly arose from my slumber and sent a text to our midwife to let her know Katie was well underway in her labor. She asked if we wanted her there ASAP. I asked her to wait for a couple of hours because I didn't want her to infringe upon one of the last dates Katie and I would be having for a while. Things were just starting to heat up.

The midwife, along with her assistant, arrived at 7 AM. They checked Katie's dilation to find that she was at a 7.5.

That number meant nothing to me. Was it a scale of one to one hundred? Was it supposed to get smaller like a countdown to liftoff? Was this number a reflection of my performance as a husband? I didn't ask. I had gotten this far in life living by the term, "fake it 'til you make it," and I wasn't about to change.

About the time the midwives arrived, Katie began to experience dramatic agony. The midwives seemed to disappear as soon as they showed up. They later told me that I was doing such a good job as Katie's coach and support that they didn't want to disrupt our rhythm. I was flattered by the comment but made it clear I did not hire them to serve me with flattering speech. (But it was nice, and our midwives were awesome.)

The next two hours were intense. Katie went from sweating like a pig to shivering like a shiverer every three minutes. She was a champ. Katie resisted the urge to fight her contractions. She let her body do what it was created to do in this scenario. She stayed relaxed even though she was experiencing greater pain than ever before. Then my world got wacky.

It was almost 9 AM.

Katie called for the midwife and said she felt like the baby was pounding on the door. In reality, our baby was about to blow a hole through the door. (I refer to it as "the door" to make this story appropriate for all ages. I know what it's really called.)

Katie leaned back on the bed. I didn't want to look, but I knew I needed to. I saw my baby's head! "Oh, my word! It's coming, Katie!"

Katie pushed. But not for long. I saw the whole head come out and turned quickly to tell Katie the news. When I turned back, the entire human body of our child had slid through the door like a wet fish. I broke down crying. Katie was sobbing tears of joy. The angelic and ever so helpful midwife skillfully placed our child on Katie's breast, and it wasn't until a stream of urine shot straight up in the air that I realized the gender.

WE HAD A BOY!!! Leon Tucker Voetberg.

Katie and I laid there in complete bliss. This was indeed the best date ever!

Katie:

Isn't my husband hilarious? Some people have taken offense for me because of Elisha's slapstick humor. But that is one of the things I love most about him, and I encourage it every chance I get. In fact, I begged Elisha to let me use this narration of our first birth in my book.

If you read the men's version of *After the Baby*, (because goodness knows if you're like me, you peek in all of your husband's books), you'll find the same dry humor and overkill descriptions. He wrote it all with my blessing and encouragement! We've shared so many good laughs over his melodramatic perspective, and I want you to know he adores me, and I know it.

But enough of the jokes. Let's dive into the nitty gritty and help you create your ideal experience once the baby arrives.

Chapter 3

Great Expectations

Splish. Splash.

Long strands of creamy milk streamed into the bucket, as Klarabelle munched calmly on her grain. Snow drifted down outside the barn, but our cow's sweet hide warmed my face as I leaned close and squeezed methodically. Left. Right. Left. Right. My 15-month-younger sister and I giggled and chatted blindly across from each other . . .

"Now you try it." A harsh voice snapped me back to reality as a wizened woman abruptly grabbed my hand and showed me how to "self-express." All those years of milking a cow had done nothing to prepare me for what I now faced. What little dignity I still had after birthing a child was now completely stripped away . . . along with nearly all my clothing.

Awkwardly, I tried to copy what the lactation consultant had been doing a moment before, but I couldn't get a drop of milk to come out of my own body.

"I bet I can do it."

Elisha's brow furrowed in deep concentration as he steadily squeezed my breastmilk onto a spoon. Three days earlier we had been passionately making love, and now my husband was only focused on his form, as he steadily relieved my engorgement. I might as well move to the barn.

Nothing can totally prepare you for what to expect postpartum. There are so many unknowns and so many unexpected changes once that little human enters the world. Even if you've already had one child, baby #2 can create an entirely new experience!

Whether this is your very first time becoming a mom or you're a seasoned veteran, chances are, your struggles postpartum are going to be similar: sleep deprivation, healing, body insecurity, lack of sex, expectations, caring for yourself, keeping a tiny human alive, juggling hormones . . . and somehow our marriages are supposed to be on that list!

So, how can we bring a blessed baby into the world without tearing down the union that created this child in the first place? How can our spouses help? How can we help them?

The bad news: our spouse still won't be able to read our minds.

The good news: Postpartum doesn't have to tear

our marriages apart! It CAN be a beautiful time that draws us together.

It just won't happen without thought and effort.

It's better you prepare your husband for your dreams of cloth diapering (and his willingness to help change them) before you're both sleep deprived and poop is pouring out of a leg hole. It's also better your husband lets you know he thought "no sex" just meant, "no intercourse," but of course you're going to, you know, find other options.

Do you plan on your mom moving in after the baby? Is there no way on earth he's going to let that happen?

Before the baby. Before emotions get out of whack. Before the beautiful, terrifying, eye-opening chaos of postpartum . . . that's the time to ask these questions.

Sure, you're still going to have to "wing it." You're still going to need to adjust to the ever- changing landscape of each postpartum, but NOW is the time to communicate your expectations surrounding whatever you deem is a "big deal." It's also time to ask a few questions to determine whether or not you're even on the same page on things you might be taking for granted.

I wish I had explicitly discussed how we were going to spend Quality Time after our first son was born. As in love as I was with Leon, I treasured the moments I had alone with my husband, and suddenly, every waking and sleeping moment had our precious son stealing the attention. I already felt unattractive, unwanted, and insecure. (I considered changing my name to Klarabelle.) It seemed Elisha's affection had transferred to our child, and I was reduced from Lover to saggy-emotional-nurse-maid. Of course, Elisha still loved me, but we both didn't grasp the importance of me feeling romanced, after the baby.

Another question I wish we had asked, was, "How do you expect to transition back into normal life?" We had no game plan and this created a lot of tension in our marriage.

I thrive on structure, deadlines, and clear goals, but days faded into weeks after Leon was born. To make it worse, Elisha and I were both self-employed at the births of our first two children. There was no way I could fully embrace resting, knowing there was no timeline for me to be on my own when Elisha returned to work. Instead, I stressed and became anxious each day I saw Elisha caring for me or our kiddos, instead of returning to work. Where was the money going to come from if we were both busy with babies? When was the end of this muddled season of days and nights swirling together in one giant mix of nursing, sweat, snuggles and tears?

Looking back, I should have trusted my husband who has always provided abundantly for our family. But another thing that would have made this easier was talking through my expectations of when postpartum would end.

Like I mentioned earlier, depending on healing, medical struggles, or Baby's unique personality, my game plan might be dismantled. But at least Elisha and I would be on the same page with what our ideal expectations were. We'd be a team.

Okay, so enough about us.

ACTION:

Grab your hubby (Elisha already prepared him to ask these same questions of you) and jot down his answers to these questions. He can jot down yours! As you go, mark with a star one or two expectations you want to communicate more in-depth.

Bonus points: Make it a date!

KATHRYN VOETBERG

25 Questions to Ask Your Spouse

1. What does God say about children? Do we believe that?

2. What role do you see your parents playing in our lives after the baby is born?

3. How much help do we want? From whom?

4. Will we circumcise?

5. What are your expectations for the labor and delivery process?

6. How earth-friendly are we going to be? Cloth diapers? Breastfeeding?

AFTER THE BABY

Before You Go Into Labor

7. How do you feel about kids sleeping in our room/bed?

8. What are THREE things we'll do to keep our relationship strong?

9. What do you see as your role during the first six months after baby is born?

10. What do you see as my role in the first six months?

11. Who are you comfortable with watching our child? Church nursery? Daycare? Babysitting?

12. How can I show you love when sex is off the table?

Continued . . .

13. What are some practical ways to help you deal with the stress of a major change?

14. What are your expectations for the first six weeks?

15. What are your expectations for our transition back into "normal" life after healing?

16. What are your thoughts about the concept of a stay at home mom?

17. When do you think you'll be comfortable leaving the baby for a date night?
For an overnight?

AFTER THE BABY

Continued . . .

18. Do you feel our marriage is ready to take on new strains, or should we look into taking a marriage course, going to a conference, or getting counseling for marriage fortification before the baby arrives?

19. What are your thoughts on family size?

20. What is one way we will spend quality time with each other after the baby is born?

21. If postpartum depression is an issue after birth, what is our game-plan? Do we have money set aside to invest into supplements? Help? Therapy? Or other means of support?

22. Who will get up for night-time feedings?

23. What are your thoughts/feelings about sleep-training?

24. So, since we can't have sex for the first few weeks, what IS on the table? Can we still fool around? Is oral sex potentially an option?

25. What baby equipment do you feel is "necessary?" What is optional?

Now that you've gone through the questions, you probably realize a couple of these need to be translated to your spouse in more depth.

Enter: *The Expectation Translator*

We're going to give you a lot of tools in this workbook, but this is hands down my favorite. We are going to use it in every, single. chapter. from here on out.

Miscommunication and unsaid (and therefore unmet) expectations are two of the biggest struggles in marriage, so we're going to do our best to clarify anything we can up front--before the baby.

You'll notice the first tool is already filled out. That's because I give you a real-life example of how I used *The Expectation Translator* to communicate my expectations of postpartum before our third child. Elisha did the same thing and we compared notes to compromise.

If you've already been through this baby rodeo before, we're giving you a bonus tool. In the back of this book, you'll find *The History Reflector*. Write down what worked the first time, what didn't work, and steps you and your spouse can take to make this time better.

For you newbies, you'll get a chance to fill this out at the end of your postpartum journey, but for now, let's focus on *The Expectation Translator*. This is going to be helpful for your marriage in general.

Here's to great conversation and the beginning of a unified vision of parenthood!

ACTION:

Fill out ONE Expectation Translator with your overall vision for postpartum, and compare notes with your hubby. Now, take the one or two areas you marked with a star up above during the "25 Questions," and fill out an Expectation Translator for both of those areas. It's okay if these are different from the expectations your husband wanted to communicate to you. Again, compare notes.

The Expectation Translator

WHAT IS YOUR GOAL?	WHAT ARE 5 THINGS YOU WANT TO BE TRUE OF THIS EXPERIENCE?
To have a smooth postpartum	1. I want to exclusively breastfeed
WHAT DOES THE IDEAL OUTCOME LOOK LIKE?	2. I want to stay in bed with nothing on the agenda for 7 days.
Elisha and I being on the same page and still finding time for each other. My body having what it needs to rest. A lot of concentrated help in the beginning so I'm able to get back on my feet.	3. I want my mom to come help for the first week
WHAT DOES THE WORST-CASE SCENARIO LOOK LIKE?	4. I want to get up at nights with the baby and have Elisha take them in the morning.
Elisha and I becoming disjointed and upset. Hurting my body by doing too much in the beginning. Stretching out the postpartum phase for weeks. Not getting on a regular schedule with work and life balance in the first 6 weeks	5. I want to start transitioning back into normal life as soon as possible

The Expectation Translator

WHAT IS YOUR GOAL?

WHAT DOES THE IDEAL OUTCOME LOOK LIKE?

WHAT DOES THE WORST-CASE SCENARIO LOOK LIKE?

WHAT ARE 5 THINGS YOU WANT TO BE TRUE OF THIS EXPERIENCE?

1

2

3

4

5

The Expectation Translator

WHAT IS YOUR GOAL?

WHAT DOES THE IDEAL OUTCOME LOOK LIKE?

WHAT DOES THE WORST-CASE SCENARIO LOOK LIKE?

WHAT ARE 5 THINGS YOU WANT TO BE TRUE OF THIS EXPERIENCE?

1.

2.

3.

4.

5.

The Expectation Translator

WHAT IS YOUR GOAL?

WHAT DOES THE IDEAL OUTCOME LOOK LIKE?

WHAT DOES THE WORST-CASE SCENARIO LOOK LIKE?

WHAT ARE 5 THINGS YOU WANT TO BE TRUE OF THIS EXPERIENCE?

1

2

3

4

5

KATHRYN VOETBERG

Chapter 4
Communication

Growing up, we called it "airspace."

It was a valuable thing in a family of 11 talkative and opinionated kids, and it was rare you'd get two words in before someone would start talking over you, especially around the dinner table. After I got married, my siblings said there was a lot more "airspace" to go around, but I think they secretly missed the intense discussions I'd bring to the table.

I was the girl that said just about every word that popped into my head— irrational thoughts, passionate feelings, chaotic emotions.

My uncle said it best, "Sometimes I wonder . . . what's Katie thinking? Oh! There it is!"

In my family, we didn't struggle with getting the words out; the problem was we said too much. We were quick to apologize and ask forgiveness, but I learned the hard way that some words you can't take back.

I still see the pain in Elisha's eyes when I think

of a conversation we had postpartum with baby number two. To this day it is still a raw wound I try to sidestep around. Although Elisha forgave me and we moved on in our relationship, I created a hole in his armor. I barely bump that sore spot and the stitches holding it closed will rip right open. We didn't get angry. It wasn't a fight.

But I thoughtlessly said how I "felt" during that emotionally tumultuous time. I thought we "needed" to have a conversation when we actually needed more sleep, and as a result, I brought up a discussion that crippled Elisha's confidence.

Tearing down our husband's confidence is one of the most hurtful things we can do to them. So many men appear macho, but underneath they struggle feeling like a fraud . . . they fear being a failure. As Elisha's wife, he needs to know I believe in him, that I have his back, that he can do anything he sets his mind to. When I have confidence in him, he has confidence in himself. It just takes a few thoughtless words to have a devastating effect.

It's a blessing we can learn and grow through these experiences. I never realized how important it was for me to voice my belief in my husband's abilities, but this one discussion drove that point home in a way I'll never forget throughout a lifetime of marriage.

God is so good, and I never want to fear communicating. However, I do want to add tools to my toolbox for emotionally foggy times.

Tool #1: THE FIRST TOOL IS MORE A RULE

There are certain things we DON'T talk about postpartum.

1. Jobs
2. Housing
3. Moving

After you have a kiddo, your whole life changes and sometimes you feel you need to change everything else, too! Take a second to imagine my mindset post baby number two.

"Yikes! I haven't showered for a week, the kids are fighting, no one is wearing real clothes, and we're relying on meals from neighbors! Something NEEDS TO CHANGE! We need more money! More help! Fewer kids!"

Obviously, that's no way to live life. It sounds like mayhem over at the Voetberg house (and it was). But gradually, it doesn't take three hours to button everyone's diapers to get out of the house. By some miracle, I start cooking again and one morning my eyelashes appear with mascara. It's like watching a one-year-old trying to figure out a spoon. It takes 100% focus, yet despite intense effort, half the applesauce falls off on the way to his mouth, and the other half slides sadly down the bib before metal reaches the toothless end zone.

Today, did you even think of your spoon when

you were eating? How about your finger placement when you picked up a pencil? This juggling act of parenthood is going to become second nature, so give it time to normalize before you jump into making (or even talking about) any drastic life-changes.

Tool #2: WORD MATCH

Have you ever just wanted to have a good cry and you don't know why? Do you ever ask your husband how he's doing and he says, "fine."

This is where *Word Match* comes in. It's an incredible tool that can help us explain ourselves to our spouse and encourage our spouse to open up to us.

For me, postpartum was just like one giant period. I was emotional, but for the first time I didn't know how I felt. I didn't know what to tell Elisha, and yet I needed, so badly, for him to understand me. Similarly, Elisha didn't know how to communicate his feelings about being a new father and husband. He was stressed, but I couldn't tell if he was stressed about the baby, upset with our lives in general, or mad at me.

Word Match isn't just a great tool to have in your postpartum toolbox. It's an incredible resource to communicate with your spouse any time you don't know what to say.

ACTION:

Ask your spouse today to point to three words to describe how they are feeling right now. Switch places, and point to three words that currently describe your emotions.

Print off this tool and use it often.

Word Match

HAPPY, cheerful, trusting, elated, confident, grateful, joyful, lighthearted, thrilled, relieved, satisfied, secure, comfortable

LOVING, affectionate, cozy, passionate, romantic, sexy, warm, tender, responsive, thankful, appreciative, refreshed

ENERGETIC, excited, rejuvenated, talkative, pumped, motivated, driven, determined, playful, optimistic

ANXIOUS, uneasy, nauseated, nervous, scared, overwhelmed, worried, stressed, smothered, paralyzed

ANGRY, annoyed, grumpy, controlled, manipulated, furious, provoked, frustrated, resentful, bitter, offended

TIRED, exhausted, burned out, overwhelmed, indifferent, detached. depressed, stretched too thin, teary, drained, sleepy

ALONE, isolated, avoidant, lonely, abandoned, deserted, cut-off, forgotten. unneeded, unappreciated, worthless

SAD, unhappy, crushed, dejected, depressed, desperate, grieved, heartbroken, heavy, weepy, disappointed, pessimistic, discontent

ASHAMED, guilty, mortified, humiliated, embarrassed, exposed, sorry, apologetic, regretful, self-conscious, confused

HURT, betrayed, bitter, broken, degraded, humiliated, rejected, scorned, squashed, wounded, belittled, insulted, insignificant, inferior, mistreated, jealous

AFRAID, scared, apprehensive, burdened, fearful, panicky, tense, terrified, insecure, worried

PEACEFUL, at ease, calm, comforted, relaxed, thoughtful

Tool #3: THE SCALE OF 1-10

This basic communication tool is super versatile, and in less than 10 seconds allows you to gauge how your spouse is truly feeling. It immediately lets you know if you're on the same page, AND it's an excellent indicator of what actions need to take place to create an even better relationship!

You hear horror stories of women snapping in postpartum because their husband says, "I'm tired," and she doesn't feel he's been a lick of help. I've cracked a time or two because Elisha and I had completely different feelings about a situation.

When using the scale of 1 to 10 in it's most basic form, you want to ask your spouse how they would rate your marriage, but in reality, you can use this tool to measure anything.

"On a Scale of One to Ten, 10 being the absolute best place we've ever been, and two being totally

lame, where would you rate our marriage, right now?"

On the Scale of One to Ten, 10 is the absolute, highest of highs: for instance, when you're in Maui, the sun is setting, and your spouse has spoiled you rotten all day, or after a reeeeallly good intimate experience, or when you look at each other and think, "I am so in love it hurts."

We don't live in the ten zone. No couple lives in the ten zone. But a good marriage can achieve those all-time highs. If you haven't had an all-time high in a couple of years, maybe it's time to put some effort into getting there.

The sweet spot is from seven to eight. This is where happy marriages live a lot of the time. Couples living in the sweet spot have disagreements, but they don't hold grudges. They're content in marriage but capable of upping the ante every once in a while to hit that colossal ten!

Then, there's any number under five, for some it's -200, for some it's two. Any number under five means you're on the rocks. It could just be a bad day at work. It could be hormones. It could be a child's doctor appointment. But for whatever reason, your spouse is emotionally fried. We want to leave this zone as soon as possible, but the good news is all marriages hit the rocks.

When your spouse says, "two," it doesn't mean you have a failing marriage. It doesn't mean you're headed for divorce. All it means is that you're at two right now. That's it. You have a starting point, and sometimes it just takes a small action to change that number in a big way.

That leads us to our second question.

"What is one thing I can do to make it better?"

The key word here is "BETTER." If your spouse just said -200, and you say, "What can I do to get us to a ten?" They aren't going to know the answer. (And if they do, chances are, it's going to be so overwhelming you aren't going to want to hear it.) With "better" they only need to come up with one baby step. Maybe you haven't had an all-time high in a couple years, or maybe they need a good night's sleep. Perhaps they need to feel heard. Be completely open to giving them whatever they need. Your spouse is giving you the road map to creating an incredible marriage!

One last reminder: it's totally possible to jump from two to ten in the same day, so don't be discouraged by whatever number your spouse gives. And secondly, don't be surprised if your spouse's number is way different from the number you would choose. Trust us. It happens all the time.

ACTION:

Ask your spouse, "On a Scale of One to Ten, 10 being the absolute best place we've ever been, and one being totally lame, where would you rate our marriage right now?"

Follow up with:
"What is ONE thing I can do to make it better?"

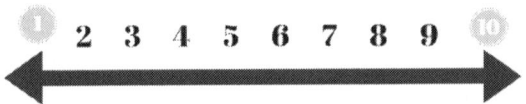

Chapter 5

Rollercoaster: Emotions and Hormones

"Katie," Elisha looked at me with horrifying visions of a perpetually sobbing wife racing through his brain, "you have to learn to not let this stuff affect you so much."

I could see his dark eyes picturing me sobbing through the rest of our, Lord willing, 60 years of marriage, and I cried even louder. "This isn't me!" My voice was muffled in his shirt. "This isn't going to be me for the rest of our lives. The midwife said I might be hormonally imbalanced for the next few weeks."

Elisha grabbed me a little tighter, and I could hear the nervousness in his voice, "What does that mean?"

Emotions and hormones can be crazy things. After Leon was born I remember bawling because Elisha was leaving for work, bawling because I couldn't find a cheese stick in the refrigerator, and bawling because I was so in love with my first child.

Elisha was a trooper, but it stressed me out that he thought his wife was never going to be the same. (And inwardly I was wondering the same thing.)

Every woman experiences some emotional upheaval while her body is flipping from baby-maker to milk-machine, to healing genie: It could be the baby blues to postpartum depression, to anxiety, or suicidal thoughts.

Here is the good news. Like everything else in life, this is a season. It ends. But there are some ways we can try to minimize the effects this emotional rollercoaster has on our health and the health of our marriage. The biggest game-changers for us were nutrition and communication.

Nutrition

This is a BIGGIE. The health of our body plays a huge role when it comes to the health of our minds. Whether or not you were supplementing through pregnancy can affect how depleted your body is once that little one comes earth side. Maybe you're breastfeeding and continuing to pour out the last of your body's nutritional reserves. On top of that, you're trying to heal and pull the sags, tears, stretches, and muscles somewhat back to normal. For most women, this process requires some help.

After my first, I learned about the power of Omega three's on the brain. Even though I vigilantly took a high-quality fish oil throughout my pregnancy, it wasn't enough for me to skip the baby blues entirely. My breastmilk contained DHA, an essential fatty acid found in fish, and since my body can't create DHA (we have to eat it) I couldn't keep replenished!

With Lucy, my second, I took the only fish oil on the market with all eight Omega threes, a concentrated form. I also took the purest one I could find-tested for over 200 toxins with an allowable limit of zero parts per billion!! There were no warning labels on the back, and I wasn't at risk for ingesting any heavy metals and toxins.

After birth I ramped up my intake from one to three capsules a day (you may even want to try up to six capsules depending on how you feel).

Was I still a little teary, tired, and impatient? Yes. But there was no hysterical bawling, no days of feeling a heavy weight in the pit of my stomach, no times of blankly staring at the wall not caring about the world around me. In short, I had a much better emotional season when it came to postpartum . . . mainly because of some pure, highly-concentrated fish oil.

Whole food nutrition is not a drug, so each body is going to respond differently. It's a great start to naturally address some of the physical strain our bodies go through during this season.

I'll give you a full list of what I take while pregnant and postpartum to provide me with energy, stamina, and hormonal balance. These are the supplements my mom has taken for over 20 years to support her body through the birth of eleven children (and she made postpartum look easy). You can order or learn more at www.nowthatwereafamily.com/afterthebaby

On our website, you can find another incredible resource for overall postpartum health--my friend's postpartum course! She's a doula and mom of seven, and her wisdom is worth hearing.

THE DAILY SUPPLEMENTS

The ProVitality Pack

- Tre-en-en
Stabilizes hormones, improves energy, allows your body to absorb 50% more nutrients from what you're already eating.

- Carotenoid Complex
Reduces oxidation, boosts immunity 37%, helps develop baby's eyesight (the equivalent of taking 85 pounds of raw fruits and vegetables a month).

- Omega III Salmon Oil Plus
Reduces inflammation, develops baby's brain and eyesight, balances hormones, improves mood.

> **- Multi Vitamin**
> 24 essential vitamins and minerals.
>
> **For leg cramps (or if this isn't your first baby)**
>
> **- Cal - Mag**
> The average absorption rate for calcium is 3- 5%, This Cal-Mag has an 85% absorption rate.
>
> **- Protein shake**
> Balances hormones, balances blood sugar.

For a discount code on Angie's Postpartum course or more nutritional information, visit: www.nowthatwereafamily.com/afterthebaby.

Communication

    Yes, we've already had a chapter on this, but I really can't mention communication enough. You can plan all you want, but you've also got to expect the unexpected. Regardless of how well you talked through your birth plan and how you were going to support each other, life is guaranteed to throw some curve balls.

Whether this is your first baby or you've gone through this rodeo several times, you never know if your child is going to be chill or a screaming spider monkey. You don't know if he'll have colic, get a rash, struggle with breastfeeding, react to a medication . . . life with children has a lot of variables. On top of that, sleep deprivation is the real deal.

There's no way we can totally rule out emotional upheaval and the potential of depression or anxiety rearing their ugly heads, but we can work through every new and unexpected factor together, as a team. This can be an incredible way to grow in unity and achieve new levels of understanding and intimacy. Knowing that your spouse has your back, is one of the most precious gifts in the world, and you want to be your spouse's biggest advocate.

Your husband isn't the enemy when things go wrong. You guys are a team. You are going to get to the other side of this, look at each other, and think, "You. Are. Awesome. We did it!"

That said, we need to utilize a few tools already in our tool belt, and add one more.

Tool #1: THE SCALE OF 1 TO 10 (LEVEL TWO)

We want you to get good at using this tool so that you will readily refer to it in helter-skelter times. In the communication chapter we already discussed the basics of how to use this, so now we're moving on to *Level Two*.

For this exercise we are going to cover the top

five things you need from your spouse and the top five things he needs from you, according to a study by Willard E. Harley Jr in his popular book, *His Needs, Her Needs*. Not only is this great practice for creatively using the 1-10 scale, but these are awesome things to keep in mind all the time. (Let's not hold ourselves to too high of a standard for this stuff during the postpartum season, though. Okay? I wouldn't dare ask Elisha to rate me on my attractiveness right after a baby . . . or our sex life . . . or domestic support . . . or really any of these. I can still admire him, but that's about it.)

If you aren't familiar with these ways we feel loved and needed by our spouse, Elisha and I break them down in episode 014 on the "Now That We're a Family Podcast," but for the most part they are pretty self-explanatory!

HIS NEEDS
1. SEX
2. RECREATIONAL COMPANIONSHIP
3. AN ATTRACTIVE SPOUSE
4. DOMESTIC SUPPORT
5. ADMIRATION

Her Needs
1. Affection
2. Conversation
3. Openness and Honesty
4. Financial Support
5. Family Leadership

ACTION:

First, rate how well you think your spouse is doing at fulfilling your needs. DON'T SHOW YOUR SPOUSE YOUR PAPER. Next, ask your spouse how well THEY believe they are doing at meeting your needs. Circle their answers on your sheet.

HIS NEEDS, *HER* NEEDS

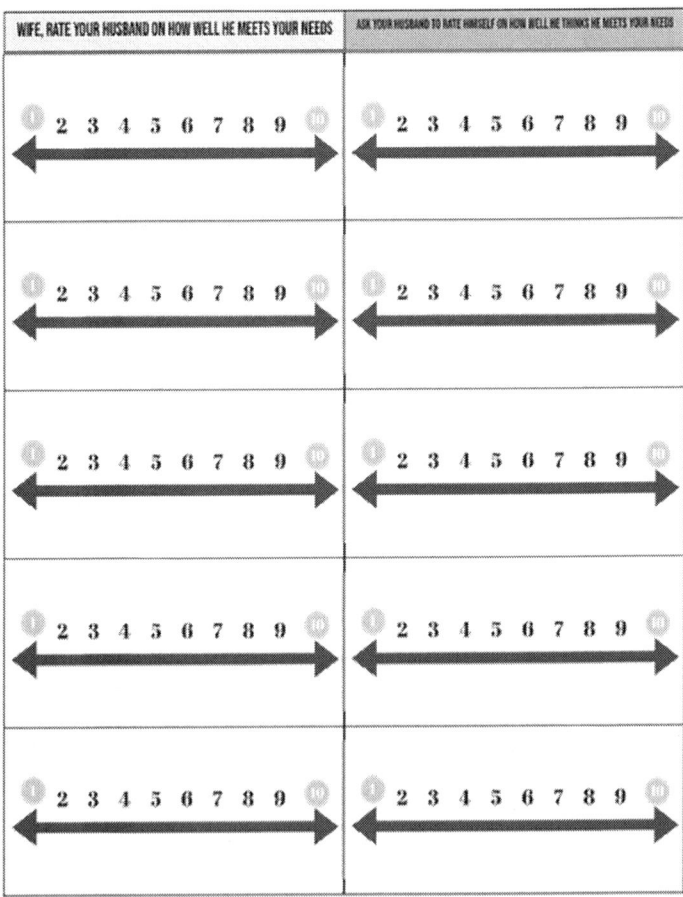

HIS NEEDS, *HER* NEEDS

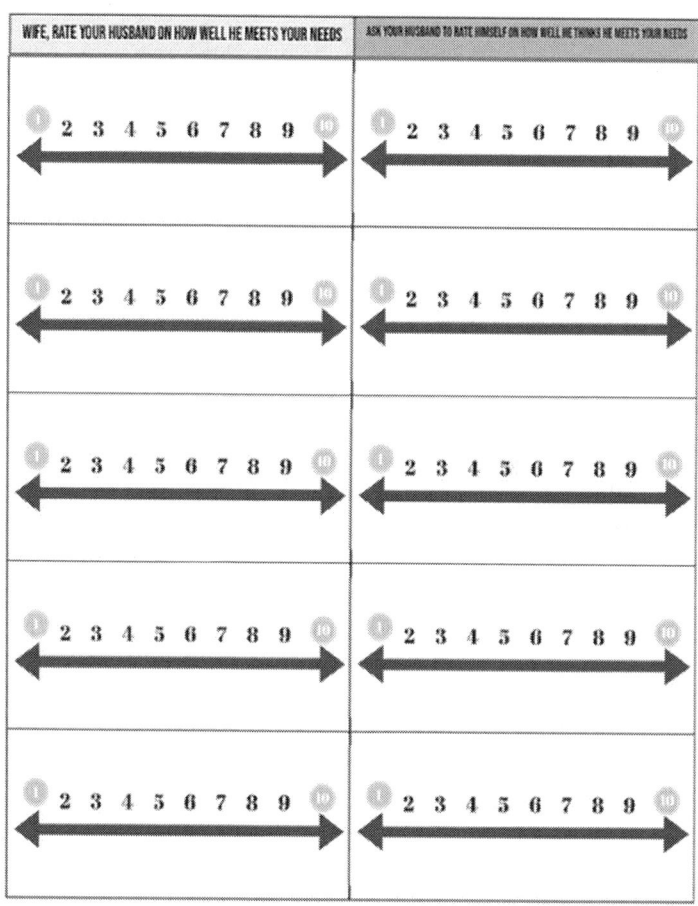

When you have finished filling out your tool and you share your answers with each other, keep two things in mind:

1. Your spouse is just giving you a number, a way to improve. Don't stress if it's lower than you thought! It's only a number, not an indicator of your marriage as a whole.

2. Remember, your spouse isn't responsible for making your marriage glorious . . . you are. Marriage isn't a 50/50 relationship where we are constantly wondering if our spouse is meeting us in the middle. A fantastic marriage is 100% our responsibility.

> Some questions to ask after the baby are: How are you feeling about being a parent on the scale of 1 to 10? How do you feel about your mental health on a scale of 1 to 10?

Tool #2: WORD MATCH (LEVEL TWO)

We covered this in the communication section as well, but don't underestimate how powerful this tool can be. Right now, we are going to use it to discover how they are feeling about the future. We're going to see how they are feeling about this upcoming season of "after the baby."

Word Match

HAPPY, cheerful, trusting, elated, confident, grateful, joyful, lighthearted, thrilled, relieved, satisfied, secure, comfortable

LOVING, affectionate, cozy, passionate, romantic, sexy, warm, tender, responsive, thankful, appreciative, refreshed

ENERGETIC, excited, rejuvenated, talkative, pumped, motivated, driven, determined, playful, optimistic

ANXIOUS, uneasy, nauseated, nervous, scared, overwhelmed, worried, stressed, smothered, paralyzed

ANGRY, annoyed, grumpy, controlled, manipulated, furious, provoked, frustrated, resentful, bitter, offended

TIRED, exhausted, burned out, overwhelmed, indifferent, detached. depressed, stretched too thin, teary, drained, sleepy

ALONE, isolated, avoidant, lonely, abandoned, deserted, cut-off, forgotten. unneeded, unappreciated, worthless

SAD, unhappy, crushed, dejected, depressed, desperate, grieved, heartbroken, heavy, weepy, disappointed, pessimistic, discontent

ASHAMED, guilty, mortified, humiliated, embarrassed, exposed, sorry, apologetic, regretful, self-conscious, confused

HURT, betrayed, bitter, broken, degraded, humiliated, rejected, scorned, squashed, wounded, belittled, insulted, insignificant, inferior, mistreated, jealous

AFRAID, scared, apprehensive, burdened, fearful, panicky, tense, terrified, insecure, worried

PEACEFUL, at ease, calm, comforted, relaxed, thoughtful

> **ACTION:**
>
> Ask your spouse, "Can you point to three words that communicate how you are currently feeling about having a child in a few weeks/months?"
>
> ---
>
> After discussing their answer, point to three words that describe how YOU are feeling about this upcoming season.

Tool #3: CODE RED

It's embarrassing to say now, but I spent the first few weeks after Leon's birth blowing up at Elisha. It didn't seem like he knew what to prioritize. The baby needed to be held and I'd already rocked him for hours. I'd had tiny hands touching me all day and I was jealous of Elisha's trips to work. Why was my husband meeting friends for a quick coffee when I was at home, drowning in drool and spit-up with a gigantic grandma diaper and a screaming infant?

Just re-writing these memories makes me cringe at my irrational thoughts. I mean, someone had to provide for us, and Elisha was completely unable to feed our child. Yet, postpartum hormones are the real deal, and I would freak out when Elisha seemed indifferent to what was "obviously" important. (This reaction isn't just limited to postpartum, by the way. It's just a LOT more rare during other times of life.)

So, we created a code word for when a regular request just isn't carrying much weight: X.

Now, when the kids need to go to bed, it's late, I feel nauseous, and Elisha is deep in conversation at a dinner party (after I've calmly let him know we're ready to go home . . . this is always the best option), I approach him again and slip "x" into my sentence. It's subtle. Some people think I have a slur, but Elisha knows this has just escalated to being a huge priority.

Code word "X" has massively cut down on me

acting like an irrational human to try to show my husband just how important something is to me. Likewise, Elisha can communicate when something is a big deal to him, instead of being quietly upset at a situation I'm not valuing and becoming bitter that I didn't understand the worth he placed on something.

Of course, if you overuse your code word, it won't mean anything at all. But like me, you might feel it's relieving to know you have a weighty way to tell your husband that something is super important to you. He'll be relieved you don't feel the need to have a full-blown melt-down when you need him to check on the baby in the middle of the night.

Code Red has been a good addition to the family, and it could save you a lot of emotional trauma.

P.S. "X" isn't our real word. We could tell you, but we'd have to kill you. ;)

ACTION:

Take a few minutes to come up with a few code word options that might work for you.

_____

_____

_____

_____

_____

KATHRYN VOETBERG

Chapter 6
Sleep and Fatigue

Sleepless nights and fatigue are no joke when you're a parent. They're also no joke when you take a red-eye flight. Or pull an all-nighter for college exams, or drink caffeine too close to bedtime. However, the lack of sleep surrounding postpartum is unique, because it goes on for such . . . a . . . long . . . time. It's not a rough night. It's a rough month, or two.

At that point I sleep train my kiddos—because goodness knows I'm not going through that torture any longer than I have to—but some mommies prefer to wake up and snuggle their babies during the night long past their first birthday.

In this chapter we're going to talk about the first six weeks. This is when the baby's clock is off. He is waking up throughout the night regularly to feed, and sleeping during the day. It doesn't matter if you swaddle, co-sleep, use a pacifier, or give formula, every single mommy has this lack of sleep in common.

For us women with dedicated partners, that can mean Daddy isn't getting a lot of sleep either.

Like I mentioned earlier, my first son didn't know anything about breastfeeding. I had high hopes he was spending those long months in my womb working on his nursing form, but turns out he was practicing his kickboxing in my rib cage. The weeks following his birth both of us would spend four-hour stretches in the middle of the night sweating and crying it out together. (Well, he slept and would try to nurse for two seconds. I was the one who looked like I was the lone survivor of World War III.)

Leon not only screamed at night for me to feed him—then instantly fell asleep when I tried to nurse—but he was also a total lightweight—five pounds. This made nursing even more critical because I had to get food down that little pile of knees and elbows if he was going to survive!

I don't mean to tell you my life story. (Although it is nice to tell someone how dedicated I was.)

I say this to say, the girl that needed a solid nine hours of nighttime sleep to be happy was now staying up for eight hours every night, frantically stressing over whether her baby was starving or not. We don't even need to consider out-of-whack hormones. Sleep deprivation was making me crazy.

The game plan you and your partner create before the sleep train flies off the tracks is essential to your sanity and the health of your marriage. There are options, just make sure you choose one; make sure you talk about it; make sure you fill out a

... Yep! You got it. At the end of this chapter, we'll have an *Expectation Translator* for you to fill out to communicate your expectations to your spouse. But for right now, let's talk about the options.

Sleeping is not an option.

THE NIGHT WATCHMAN

Trading off nighttime duties with your partner can work well if you're bottle feeding baby: you take one shift, they take the next. If you're exclusively pumping, feeding formula, or a combination, this can be an excellent way for your partner to spell you. By alternating feedings during the night you'll be able to sleep for a solid six hours.

THE "WHO NEEDS SLEEP?"

I don't get this one, but I don't have to. Some couples honestly work well together during every nighttime feeding. In fact, when we were pregnant with our first, a good friend encouraged Elisha to get up with me every time I breastfed. He shared that his wife would nurse and then he would burp the baby . . . give the baby back . . . his wife would finish nursing and he would burp the baby again. For him, it was bonding time with his children during the night.

Bless that man and his positive perspective on bonding, but goodness knows if Elisha and I did that we would both be at each other's throats the next day.

(This also worked for Elisha's parents because Lisa, his mom, had insomnia. Just know yourselves and how you work!)

THE 12 HOUR SHIFT

This is my personal favorite. Because I've been blessed to exclusively breastfeed my babies, I am needed every three hours, 24 hours a day. The way I see it, I'd like Elisha to be sleeping when I'm not so he's happy and energetic the next day (and has enough grace to put up with me). If you already have toddlers, I feel it's necessary to have a rested spouse to spell you the next day. I'll typically nurse throughout the night, sleep in each morning when Baby usually has his longest sleep session, and then hand our child off to Elisha. I catch naps throughout the day, and he's able to take the day shift when it comes to taking care of our little ones.

In theory, this sounds like everyone is getting enough sleep, but I love hanging out with my hubby and children during the day, so it can be a struggle to force myself to nap. Do as I say, not as I do.

When He Goes Back To Work...

One of these options might work for the first week or two, but what about when your husband goes back to work? For me, the sleep deprivation peaked at about four weeks, and Elisha was gone. My children needed me during the day, and we still weren't sleeping at night.

My biggest suggestion is get help. I didn't do this with my first. I didn't do this with my second.

I am absolutely doing this with my third.

We live in a world that encourages autonomy, and when it comes to my problems, I'm about as independent as they come. I hate asking others for help because I know some people out there don't have that option. For some reason that makes me feel guilty if I get it myself.

That said, there's no rule that it has to be you or your spouse handling every single cry, burp, and swaddle. You can be a martyr, but if there is any way you can avoid this it will be better for everyone. Bring in some refreshed eyes! Bring in some energy! If you hate feeling like a "burden," hire help!

This is what I mean by "help."

The first couple of weeks people bring you some meals, maybe your mom comes over, or someone in the community lends you a hand. (Side note: If you don't know anyone willing to support you during your first couple weeks, I would start diving deeper and create a community of real relationships. We weren't designed to be lone "Rangers.") After around week one or two the food dries up, your extra hands go home, your hubby goes back to work, and the fun is just beginning.

This is my plan for baby number three: I'm going to hire someone for one to two hours a day, five days a week during weeks three, four, and five after my delivery. I'm aiming to get someone to help me from 4-6pm every evening. The house will be thrashed, my kiddos will be hungry, Elisha will be on his way home, and I'll be pretty darn out of juice, if I figure correctly.

I looked on Care.com, and in 2019 I can get one hour worth of help a day for $200-$300 a month. For two hours a day that would be $400-$600. Depending on where you are in life, that might seem like chump change or an insurmountable saving budget. If you don't have the money, there are many ways to get it in a few weeks. Saving early is the simplest way to come up with some extra cash, but you can also create it with these short-term options.

> 1. Sell what you have (I've earned $100's that way)
> 2. Do direct sales for a couple months (make sure the commissions are at least 25%, and you love the product. I've killed it at this.)
> 3. Tutor
> 4. Ask your friends and family if they have any odd jobs
> 5. Babysit yourself (maybe babysit a few families in exchange for them coming over and helping you after your baby is born)
> 6. Do Instacart. Postmates, or Uber Eats
> 7. Sign up as a Lyft Driver
> 8. Delete monthly subscriptions
> 9. Get paid to let people borrow your car with Gets round

If you don't have the finances to afford help today, and if it's worth it to you, you'll find a way to stash some extra cash. (I'm telling you, it's worth it.)

If you do have friends and family who would be willing to help, create a schedule for yourself of what help you would love and when. Then take the time to call and line up friends or family to give an hour of their time. Whatever you do, don't leave yourself stranded in the postpartum haze of three to six weeks with no one but you or your drained husband for support-even if you just get someone to spell you once a week. I did it, lots of moms do it, and you can do it, but toughing it out is unnecessary.

Here are some ideas of what you can ask friends/family/babysitter to do:

1. Do a load of laundry
2. Tidy the house
3. Make dinner
4. Watch baby so you can nap/shower/get dressed/leave the house
5. Watch baby so you and your hubby can have alone time at home or out
6. Take your house-bound toddlers to the library
7. Take your kids on a play date
8. Clean the bathrooms

I watch a lot of moms go through postpartum depression because they are needed 100% of the time. There is no time they can look forward to relief from the constant drain of a new infant, that may or may not be colicky, happy, or a screaming werewolf.

ACTION:

Fill out an Expectation Translator of what your goal is for managing sleep and fatigue.

Do you want help? If so, who and when? Be detailed. What is your ideal schedule for trading off with the baby? Who will take the baby during the night?

Fill out your translator first, then compare notes with your husband.

The Expectation Translator

WHAT IS YOUR GOAL?

WHAT DOES THE IDEAL OUTCOME LOOK LIKE?

WHAT DOES THE WORST-CASE SCENARIO LOOK LIKE?

WHAT ARE 5 THINGS YOU WANT TO BE TRUE OF THIS EXPERIENCE?

1

2

3

4

5

Chapter 7
Intimacy During Healing

Sex. With my first, it was the last thing I wanted to think about. I thought I was trading my big tight balloon belly for myself when Leon entered the world. Boy, was I wrong. Instead, I was left with purple stretch marks racing up my flattening backside. My stomach sagged like a tarp full of water, and my breasts were so hard and engorged they took over my armpits and the remains of my neck. Dark circles ringed my raccoon eyes, and milk spurted spontaneously from my boobs every time I rolled over. Just when I thought it couldn't get any worse, Leon stopped nursing on one breast and it shriveled up like a shrunken water balloon.

I paint this picture, because when my midwife gave the six-week-go-head, I was Dolly Parton on one side, Slim Jim on the other, and a pile of scars and sagging skin. Sexy.

Now, if you're a new mom, stop. Don't freak out.

Don't have nightmares of my postpartum body or your own.

It takes time for our bodies to heal, and my post-baby body eventually morphed back into a strong, attractive, feminine physique. Another reason to not freak out is because your feelings of body insecurity and sexual drive can change with each child. You might not feel this way at all!

With Lucy, the very first night she came earth side I was raring to go. (The sunless tanner I applied before her birth probably helped. It always does.) The last two weeks before she was born I was huffing and puffing like the wolf in The Three Little Pigs, and because of Lucy's position in my belly, physical intimacy was uncomfortable and awkward. Now, suddenly, I could snuggle my jello-y belly right next to Elisha instead of being separated by a gigantic battering ram. I didn't have fears of my body returning to normal, because it shrunk back the first time and I figured it would happen again. I wasn't scared by the self-ejecting milk pumps that I'd come to love, and better yet, I knew Elisha wasn't scared away by them either. To top it off, I'd just birthed a baby, gosh, dang it! It was time to celebrate.

Needless to say, this time around Elisha didn't need to suggest other ways of physically romancing each other, and I may or may not have not waited on the midwife. (Which I can't recommend as a valid option, but sometimes desperate people do desperate things, okay?)

One thing to think about before you have a baby

is how you foresee being romanced/ romancing your partner in a sexual and non-sexual way. Let me explain what I mean when I say, "in a sexual way."

With our first, I was one fragile, hurting, bleeding, wound. Everything was painful, and I didn't want to be touched . . . at all. That was just the first couple weeks though. Eventually, I wanted to know Elisha still needed me sexually. I wanted to kiss him. I wanted to snuggle in bed and whisper in each other's ears. But I made it so clear any touching was "off limits" at the beginning of my healing, Elisha didn't initiate anything. He didn't want me to feel any pressure, and I thought my husband never wanted to be with me again. Slightly over dramatic, but 100% true.

ACTION:

Take a moment to write down your expectations when it comes to physical intimacy, romance, and date nights after the baby. Since intercourse is out of the question, are there other ways you are willing to satisfy your husband periodically? Do you expect him to initiate? Would you prefer being the only one to initiate during this season—have it be more on an, "if I feel like it," basis? How do you foresee enjoying being romanced in a sexual and non-sexual way?

The Expectation Translator

WHAT IS YOUR GOAL?

WHAT DOES THE IDEAL OUTCOME LOOK LIKE?

WHAT DOES THE WORST-CASE SCENARIO LOOK LIKE?

WHAT ARE 5 THINGS YOU WANT TO BE TRUE OF THIS EXPERIENCE?

1

2

3

4

5

Expectations don't equal reality, so make sure you and your hubby have thought through an emergency c-section, medical emergencies, or a highly needy child. Elisha and I like to expect the best, but have a game plan for the worst case scenario.

Let's say anything sexually is 100% off the table. Make sure you jot down a few ideas of simple things your husband can do to still make you feel loved and vice-versa: A love note? A love text? Do flowers mean anything to you? A small gift? Just an indication that he's thinking of you? Holding his hand? Stroking his hair? There are so many ways we can still let our spouses know we love them, and are in love with them, even in the most challenging seasons.

I know it doesn't sound sexy, but our feelings follow our actions. Meaning, if you don't feel in love, doing something a person that IS feeling in love would do, can make you feel in love.

So what do couples that "are in love" do? They touch. They go on dates. They make time for intimate conversation. They go out of their way for the other person. They tell them that they love them. The happiest marriages I see are the ones who habitually take action by doing things happy marriages do. As a result, they often feel in love.

Let's take it down from the theoretical skies of perfection and into our disheveled-topsy-turvy-sleep-deprived-living-on-freezer-meals homes. What does that look like postpartum? What does it look like when you don't have the energy to do anything, let alone think of romance?

For me, it's been helpful to preplan romantic gestures for my husband. Yep. Weeks in advance I actually take the action of planning acts of love for the postpartum season. As you roll out these surprises during those first few weeks you'll be surprised at how his love, patience, and helpfulness increases toward you. Hint: It helps if you know your husband's love language. If you don't, ask him what they may be.

We all like to receive love in specific ways, and I'm all about leveraging my impact. I mean, if I go out and spend one thousand dollars on a watch and Elisha's not a gift guy, what's the point?

It would be better if I sent him a 50 cent postcard because his love language is words of affirmation. If these terms sound like Chinese, I'll break them down quickly below. The full definitions and applications of *The 5 Love Languages* are in an excellent book by Gary Chapman. I suggest you add it to your library if you haven't already.

ACTION:

After you've determined your husband's love languages (don't be like me and try to tell him what his love languages are for him). Mark a star next to three things you can prepare ahead of time to show your spouse you love him. During the upcoming dry spell of romance, you'll be surprised at how much these little (or big) gestures can keep the spark alive!

Words of Affirmation

This person loves being loved with . . . words! Tell them they are awesome and their heart will be yours. But (as I am slowly learning) be specific and tell them often. Do you ever get tired of hearing, "you're beautiful?" I don't. You could tell me 100 times a day and it would still be music to my ears. Likewise, I have to remind myself that even though I told Elisha I admired his discipline and work ethic yesterday, and even though I thanked him for providing for us last week, he still needs to be told again!

> 1. Pre-write 6 reasons why you believe he will be a great Daddy (or why you're grateful he's your baby's daddy). Give him one a day your first 6 days (better yet, ask a friend to mail them to your house each day).
>
> 2. Pre-write a social media caption praising your spouse. (Post after the baby is born).
>
> 3. Pre-record a voice memo in your phone telling them all the things you love about them. Text it to him at work.

> 4. Write down things you appreciate your spouse in a journal. When you're tired and lacking creativity, open it up and text him one of those thoughts. Or mention one of the compliments throughout the day.
>
> 5. Burn a CD of songs that make you think of your spouse.

Acts of Service

This person loves when you do the laundry, call the plumber so they don't have to, anticipate their needs, and ask, "What can I do to help?" After three years of marriage, I finally realized this was Elisha's second love language. That's why it meant so much to him when I did the dishes. Loving a spouse with acts of service can be difficult when you have to lay in bed all day, so for baby number three, I definitely planned ahead.

One quick example: we were broke with our second child and Elisha loved to spend time at coffee shops. We got into many disagreements on whether or not to spend money on coffee.

For baby number two I stashed away a few dollars—seriously, like fifteen dollars, for him to spend on coffee. This might sound dumb. But it meant a lot that I thought of him, and he loved spending those few dollars freely, knowing I was totally supportive!

Think of his needs, even if they are little ones, and he'll love you for it.

> 1. Set aside money for him to enjoy postpartum.
>
> 2. Ask a babysitter ahead of time to be on call 2-3 weeks after your baby so you can go on a date.
>
> 3. Prepare freezer meals ahead of time, have a friend schedule a meal train, have a detailed calendar of what takeout place you'd like to have during dinner, or sign up for a meal delivery service.
>
> 4. Ask a friend/family member, (or hire someone) to come over and do the laundry and tidy the house for a couple hours your first week postpartum.
>
> 5. Schedule a night with someone to watch the kids / help you so your hubby can be free to go spend a couple hours by himself or with friends.
>
> 6. Have a small box of "his favorites" stashed away that you can pull out and give to him. For Elisha, that would be Barbecue chips, a new Vince Flynn Novel, and a bottle of one of his favorite drinks.
>
> 7. Watch something with him you might not be interested in.
>
> 8. Write him a little I.O.U. coupon book and leave a couple spots blank.

Gifts

This one seems pretty self-explanatory, but some people just like gifts in general, and others love the gift of your presence. Take the weeks leading up to postpartum to be thoughtful about what will genuinely communicate your love through a gift. After our first round of becoming parents, I knew Elisha was just as tired and frazzled as I was, so for baby number two I bought a gift card for a massage at the spa across the street from us.

> 1. Buy a gift card for a place he loves
>
> 2. Give him the gift of "alone time" and plan to have someone else help you out so he can get a break from being in "daddy-mode" 100% of the time.
>
> 3. Gift him with something he's wanted for a long-time as a "New Daddy" present.
>
> 4. Observe his habits and pick up a couple small gifts he loves. What store does he like to browse? What's his favorite flavor of gum? If I buy Elisha Reeses Peanut butter cups he's in heaven. Again, stash a little care package you can pull out and give to him later.

Quality Time

This is my love language, so I'm speaking from experience when I say having a new baby always around can be hard for the person whose love language is quality time. I wanted time for Elisha to just look into my eyes and listen to me blab, cry, or laugh, all that was on my heart. I wanted to have 30 minutes during the day when he was devoted only to me—not the baby's needs, not work, not the house. With baby number two he did an incredible job of this, and I felt so loved!

> 1. Mentally prepare yourself to leave the baby in another room, even for a few minutes and let your spouse know you're 100% dedicated to him during that time.
>
> 2. Pre-plan a short date — maybe even one hour — without the baby.
>
> 3. Suggest you go on a drive, let your new one sleep in their carseat and just talk about life.
>
> 4. Tell your spouse you WANT to spend time with them and have a couple questions pre-written to encourage conversation.

> 5. Have a babysitter—or friend and family member—lined up who would be willing to watch your newborn even upstairs or in the other room so you can fully be present with your spouse.
>
> 6. Pre-think through a list of things your husband loves, and write down a couple of these activities you may be able to share in postpartum. Maybe it's a couples massage. Maybe it's simply sitting next to him while he does something he enjoys. Maybe it's buying a new board game.

Physical Touch

Thankfully, a guy with the physical touch love language doesn't limit "physical touch" to sex. That said, sex may be more important to these men. Along with the list below, discuss how long your husband expects to wait for intercourse after the baby. Let him know what other options of sexual engagement you think you'll be open to, and find out what would mean a lot to him.

1. Write a list of small physical acts your spouse loves you to do {refer back to it when maybe you aren't feeling so touchy after baby).

2. Set an alarm on your phone to "initiate" touching your spouse. Hug them. Kiss them. Run your fingers through their hair. Maybe just hold their hand, or brush by them.

3. Ask your spouse now, what ways they enjoy being touched by you.

4. Mentally prepare to cuddle with your spouse after the baby.

Set up a cuddle date. Think of someone who would be willing to watch your baby, and plan a date to spend time just cuddling with your spouse at some point postpartum. Maybe have a box of your favorite treats pre-stashed and just go up to your room and snuggle and chat or watch something while you stroke him.

Chapter 8

We're Huge Fans of YOUR Family

We've covered a lot in this little book, both practical and tactical. But sometimes it's just as important to take a step back from the details and ask, "Why are we doing this?"

Why are the sleepless nights worth it? Why are the new pressures on our marriage beautiful and necessary? Why do we want to lean in and embrace the birth of each child?

Because God's Word tells us these little lives are a blessing. They bless our marriages by uniting our vision as parents with a common goal - to raise a child in the nurture and admonition of the Lord. They bless our souls and their presence heightens our innocence. They mirror the childlike faith we should have with our Heavenly Father. They bless us with unconditional love. As we surrender our parenting to God, they ultimately bless the world with the joy of our Creator and bring glory to Him.

Coming from a family of eleven children, with

two deeply invested parents, I can say that all of their hard work was worth it. They surrendered their desires to the Lord, and as a result, the impact they have through their children is far-reaching. My desire is to pray and work to cultivate the same deep relationships with my children that my parents created with me.

The world wants to tell you the next big career, the house, the travel. THAT'S where the joy is found. They'll tell you if you're going to have impact, you should become a lawyer, or volunteer, and put off having children so you can focus on helping society. They'll tell you children are a burden, a bump in the road, something you should just try to get to 18 and into college as soon as possible.

They'll sigh when you have a two-year-old, pity you when they're teenagers, and cheer when you let them go. But that is not embracing the blessing that is ours to enjoy!

I want to encourage you to embrace the blessing, endeavor to raise children that are a blessing, and strive to protect your mind and heart from the enemy's disgust of God's creation.

These resources have been a blessing to me on my journey of marriage and motherhood, and it is my hope they bless you as well.

- The Power of Motherhood
  - Nancy Campbell

- 100 Days of Blessing Devotional
  - Nancy Campbell

- His Needs. Her Needs - Willard Harvey

- The 5 Love Languages - Gary Chapman

- www.NowThatWereAFamily.com

- www.FamilyLifeToday.com

Bonus Tool: THE HISTORY REFLECTOR

They say hindsight is 20-20, so let's leverage that. Whether your first postpartum was complicated, or perfect—whether your most recent postpartum season is hard or incredible—you can learn from that experience!

Elisha and I love to pull out the *History Reflector* after a big event, after something we had great expectations for, after a road trip, after . . . the baby.

It's straightforward, but it eliminates us stuffing down our negative emotions and brings to light what we loved about a situation!

ACTION:
Print this out and use it all the time, haha. Seriously though, fill this out after the baby. Or, if you've already had a child, feel free to fill this out right away and see what takeaways you and your spouse have from that experience.

AFTER THE BABY

THE HISTORY REFLECTOR

I'D LIKE TO MAKE _____ BETTER

WHAT WORKED?	WHAT DID NOT WORK?

WHAT STEPS COULD I TAKE TO MAKE THIS EXPERIENCE MORE POSITIVE AND FULFILLING?

1.
2.

WHAT STEPS COULD YOU TAKE TO MAKE THIS EXPERIENCE MORE POSITIVE AND FULFILLING?

1.
2.

Don't just use this tool after the baby. Print off the *History Reflector* after each child and write down what worked, what didn't, and what you could do to make it better. Better yet, tuck it away for safe keeping, and like all the tools mentioned in this chapter, pull it out for any reason! In our experience, these little resources we shared from our toolbox help us grow deeper in love and understanding for one another.

May the Lord richly bless you through this season of childbirth and parenting! May he bless your marriage and draw you toward each other as you work to build a powerful family unit, bringing glory to him.

All my love, sweet Mama,
Kathryn Voetberg

Where you can find us

Print off copies of tools and find more resources at:
www.NowThatWereAFamily.com/afterthebaby

www.NowThatWereAFamily.com

Instagram:
@nowthatimamother
@nowthatimafather

Podcast: Now That We're A Family

Join Our weekly newsletter to hear what's happening with our own family
www.nowthatwereafamily.com/newsletter

KATHRYN VOETBERG

Made in the USA
Columbia, SC
22 June 2023

18741539R00054